Pups Help the Elephants

By Rachel Bladon

This is a camp.

Help Chase. Find the mommy elephant.

Skye can help.

🔊 2 Picture Dictionary

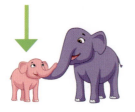 baby

 banana

 camp

 elephant

 happy

 hungry

 loud

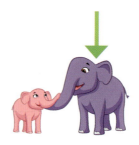 mommy

 pit

Activities

1 Match and say.

2 Find five differences.

Count all the stars in the book. ⭐